HAL•LEONARD

HARMONICA PLAY•ALONG

VOL. 6

COUNTRY Hits

Harmonica by Steve Cohen
Guitar by Mike DeRose
Bass, Keyboard, and Drums by Chris Kringel
Drums by Sean Reinert
Keyboard by Kurt Cowling

ISBN 978-1-4234-2392-8

Visit Hal Leonard Online at
**www.halleonard.com**

HAL•LEONARD®
CORPORATION
7777 W. BLUEMOUND RD. P.O. BOX 13819
MILWAUKEE, WISCONSIN 53213

## CONTENTS

# HARMONICA NOTATION LEGEND

Harmonica music can be notated two different ways: on a *musical staff*, and in *tablature*.

**THE MUSICAL STAFF** shows pitches and rhythms and is divided by bar lines into measures. Pitches are named after the first seven letters of the alphabet.

**TABLATURE** graphically represents the harmonica music. Each note will be accompanied by a number, 1 through 10, indicating what hole you are to play. The arrow that follows indicates whether to blow or draw. (All examples are shown using a C diatonic harmonica.)

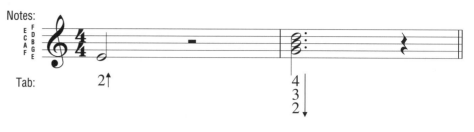

Blow (exhale) into 2nd hole.

Draw (inhale) 2nd, 3rd, & 4th holes together.

## Notes on the C Harmonica

**Exhaled (Blown) Notes**

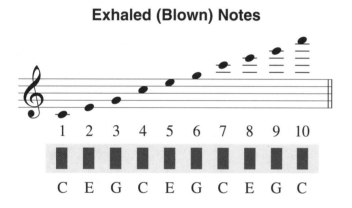

|   |   |   |   |   |   |   |   |   |    |
|---|---|---|---|---|---|---|---|---|----|
| 1 | 2 | 3 | 4 | 5 | 6 | 7 | 8 | 9 | 10 |
| C | E | G | C | E | G | C | E | G | C  |

**Inhaled (Drawn) Notes**

|   |   |   |   |   |   |   |   |   |    |
|---|---|---|---|---|---|---|---|---|----|
| 1 | 2 | 3 | 4 | 5 | 6 | 7 | 8 | 9 | 10 |
| D | G | B | D | F | A | B | D | F | A  |

## Bends

**Blow Bends**

- 1/4 step
- 1/2 step
- 1 step
- 1 1/2 steps

**Draw Bends**

- 1/4 step
- 1/2 step
- 1 step
- 1 1/2 steps

# Definitions for Special Harmonica Notation

**SLURRED BEND:** Play (draw) 3rd hole, then bend the note down one whole step.

**GRACE NOTE BEND:** Starting with a pre-bent note, immediately release bend to the target note.

**VIBRATO:** Begin adding vibrato to the sustained note on beat 3.

**TONGUE BLOCKING:** Using your tongue to block holes 2 & 3, play octaves on holes 1 & 4.

**TRILL:** Shake the harmonica rapidly to alternate between notes.

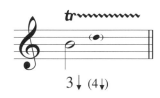

**NOTE:** Tablature numbers in parentheses are used when:

- The note is sustained, but a new articulation begins (such as vibrato), or
- The quantity of notes being sustained changes, or
- A change in dynamics (volume) occurs.
- It's the alternate note in a trill.

# Additional Musical Definitions

***D.S. al Coda***

- Go back to the sign (%), then play until the measure marked "***To Coda***," then skip to the section labelled "**Coda**."

***D.C. al Fine***

- Go back to the beginning of the song and play until the measure marked "***Fine***" (end).

  *(accent)*

- Accentuate the note (play initial attack louder).

*(staccato)*

- Play the note short.

- Repeat measures between signs.

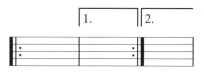

- When a repeated section has different endings, play the first ending only the first time and the second ending only the second time.

# Dynamics

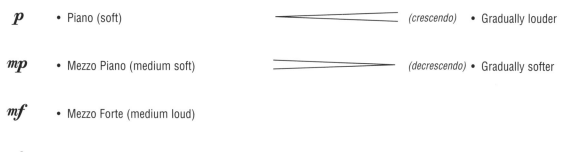

***p***
- Piano (soft)

***mp***
- Mezzo Piano (medium soft)

***mf***
- Mezzo Forte (medium loud)

***f***
- Forte (loud)

*(crescendo)* • Gradually louder

*(decrescendo)* • Gradually softer

# Ain't Goin' Down
# ('Til the Sun Comes Up)

**Words and Music by Kim Williams,
Garth Brooks and Kent Blazy**

**HARMONICA**
Player: Terry McMilan
Harp Key: C Diatonic

**Interlude**

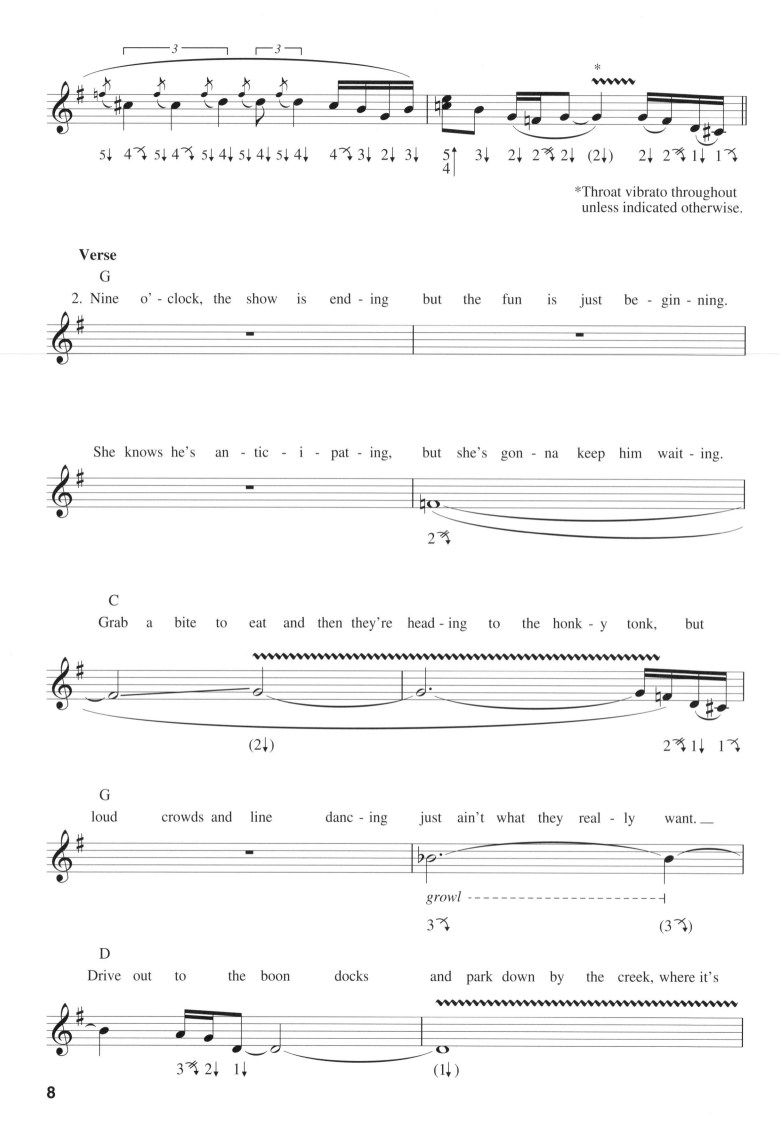

\*Throat vibrato throughout
unless indicated otherwise.

**Verse**

G

2. Nine o'-clock, the show is end - ing but the fun is just be - gin - ning.

She knows he's an - tic - i - pat - ing, but she's gon - na keep him wait - ing.

C

Grab a bite to eat and then they're head - ing to the honk - y tonk, but

G

loud crowds and line danc - ing just ain't what they real - ly want. __

*growl*

D

Drive out to the boon docks and park down by the creek, where it's

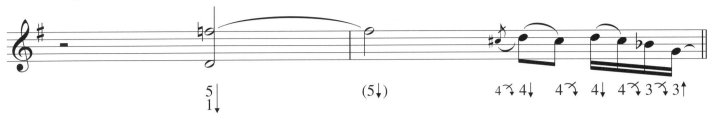

George Strait 'til real late and danc-ing cheek to cheek.

**Interlude**

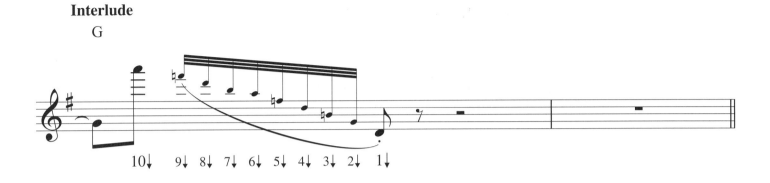

**Chorus**

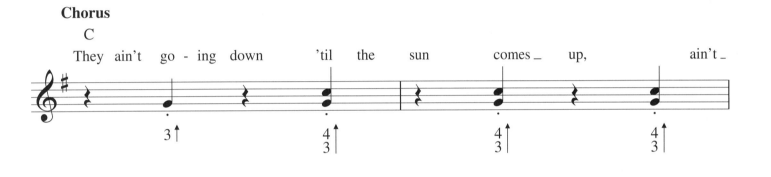

They ain't go-ing down 'til the sun comes up, ain't

giv-ing in 'til they get e-nough.

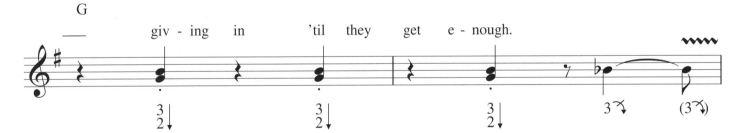

Go-ing 'round the world in a pick-up truck.

Ain't go-ing down 'til the sun comes up.

**Harmonica Solo**

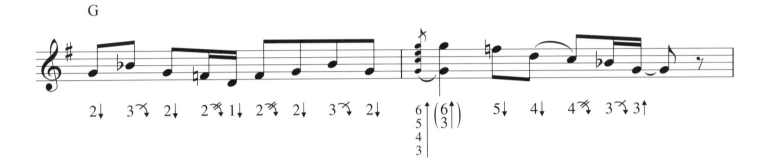

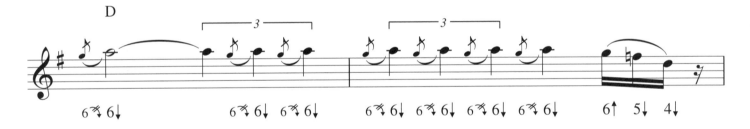

*Hand vibrato

**Bridge**

G          N.C.                              G          N.C.

Ten   to   twelve  is   wine  and  danc - in'.   Mid - night  starts  the  hard  ro - manc - in'.

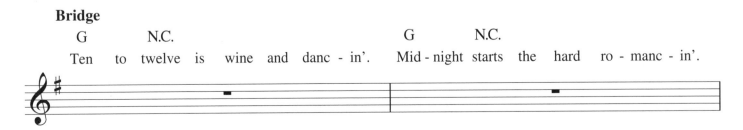

C      N.C.                   G      N.C.

One o'-clock, that truck is rock-in'. Two is com-in', still no stop-in'.

D      N.C.                   D      N.C.

Break to check the clock at three, they're right on where they wan - na be. An'

G

four o'-clock, get up, get go - in'. Five o'-clock, that roost-er's crow-in'. __

**Guitar Solo**

G

C

G                               D

**Bridge**

G

Six  o'-clock  on  Sat - ur - day,  her  folks  don't  know  he's  on  his  way.  The

stalls  are  clean,  the  hors - es  fed,  they  say  she's  gound - ed  'til  she's  dead.  Well,

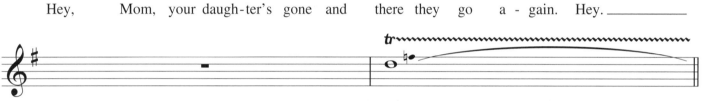

D

here  he  comes  a - round  the  bend,  slow - ing  down  she's  jump - ing  in.

G

Hey,  Mom,  your  daugh-ter's  gone  and  there  they  go  a - gain.  Hey._____

4↓ 5↓

**Guitar Solo**

G

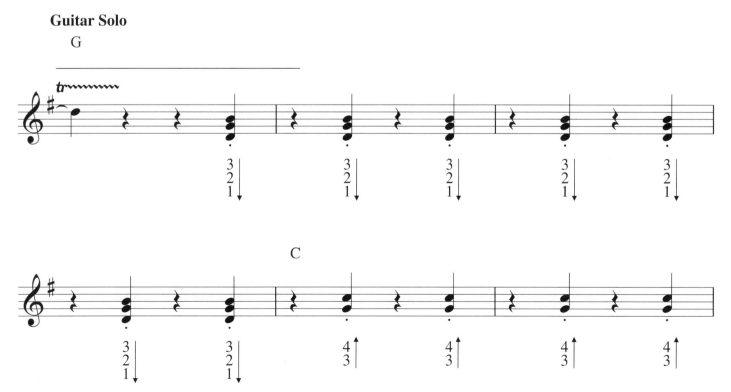

C

*Tremolo (modulate air flow w/ tongue)

(Hi-hat & drum cues)

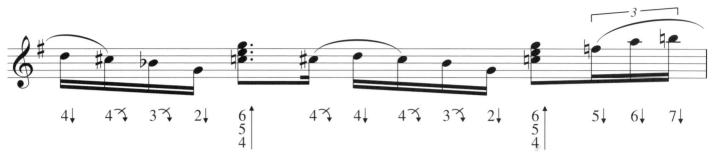

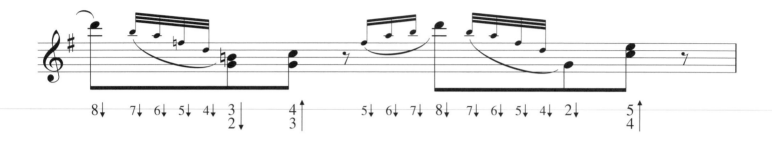

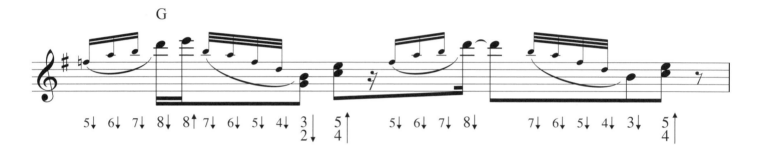

**Guitar Solo**

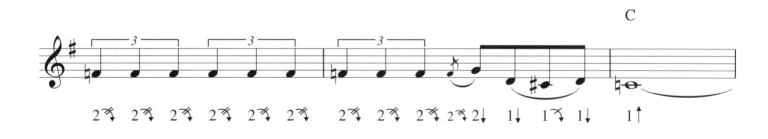

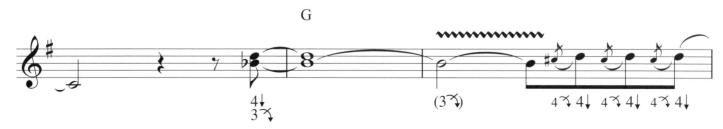

**Harmonica Solo**

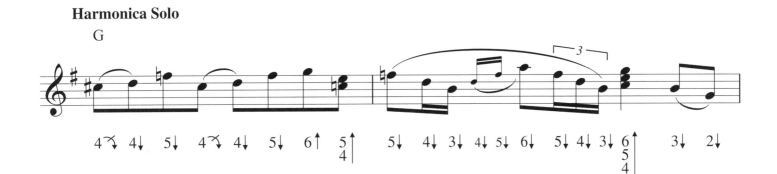

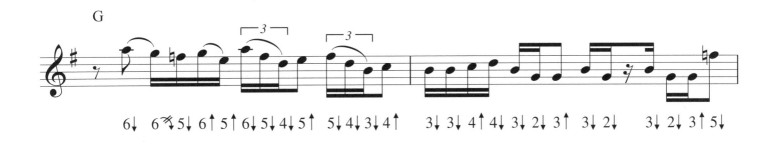

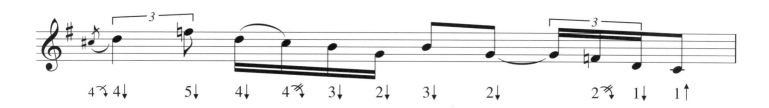

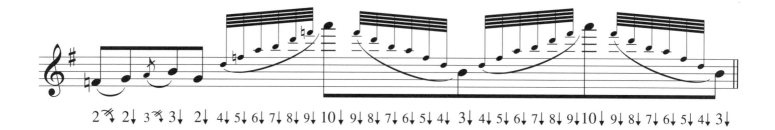

**Guitar Solo**

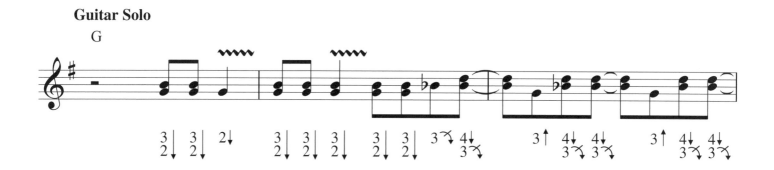

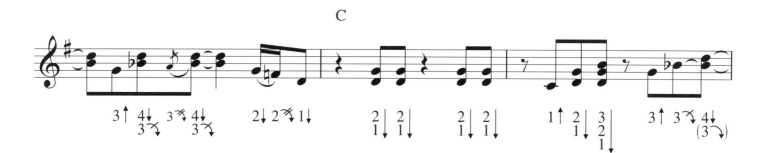

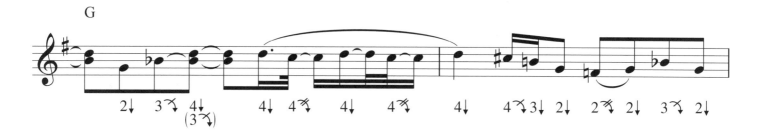

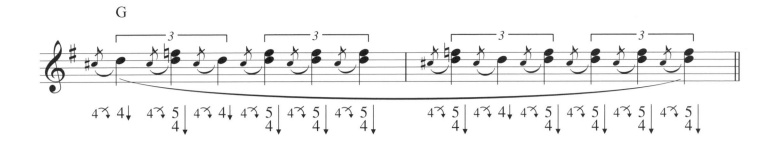

**Guitar/Harmonica Solo**
**(trading twos)**

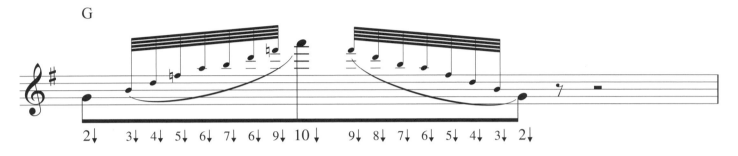

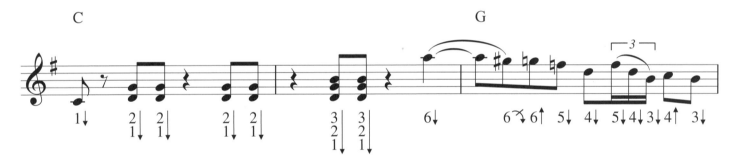

*Begin fade*

*Fade out*

# Drive
## (For Daddy Gene)

**Words and Music by Alan Jackson**

**HARMONICA**
**Player: Jim Hoke**
**Harp Key: E Diatonic**

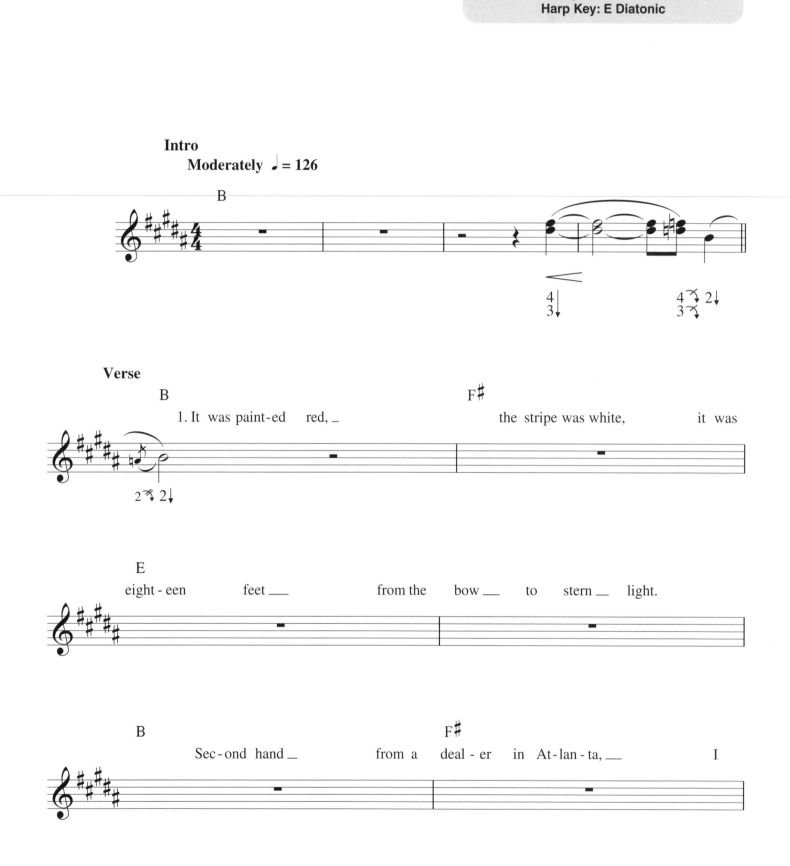

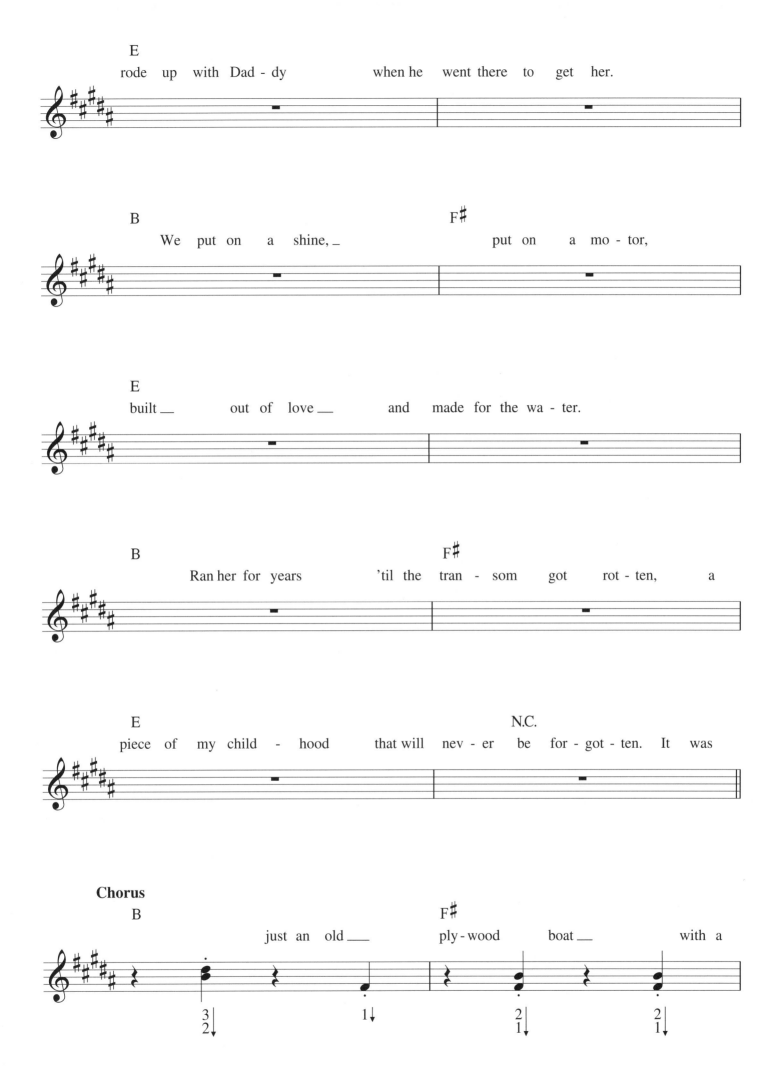

E

rode up with Dad - dy    when he    went there to    get her.

B                                F#

We  put on    a  shine, __               put on    a  mo - tor,

E

built __    out of love __    and    made for the wa - ter.

B                                F#

Ran her for years    'til the tran - som    got    rot - ten,    a

E                                N.C.

piece of  my  child - hood    that will nev - er    be  for - got - ten.  It  was

**Chorus**

B                                F#

just  an  old __    ply - wood    boat __               with a

3
2

1

2
1

2
1

*Throat vibrato throughout unless indicated otherwise.

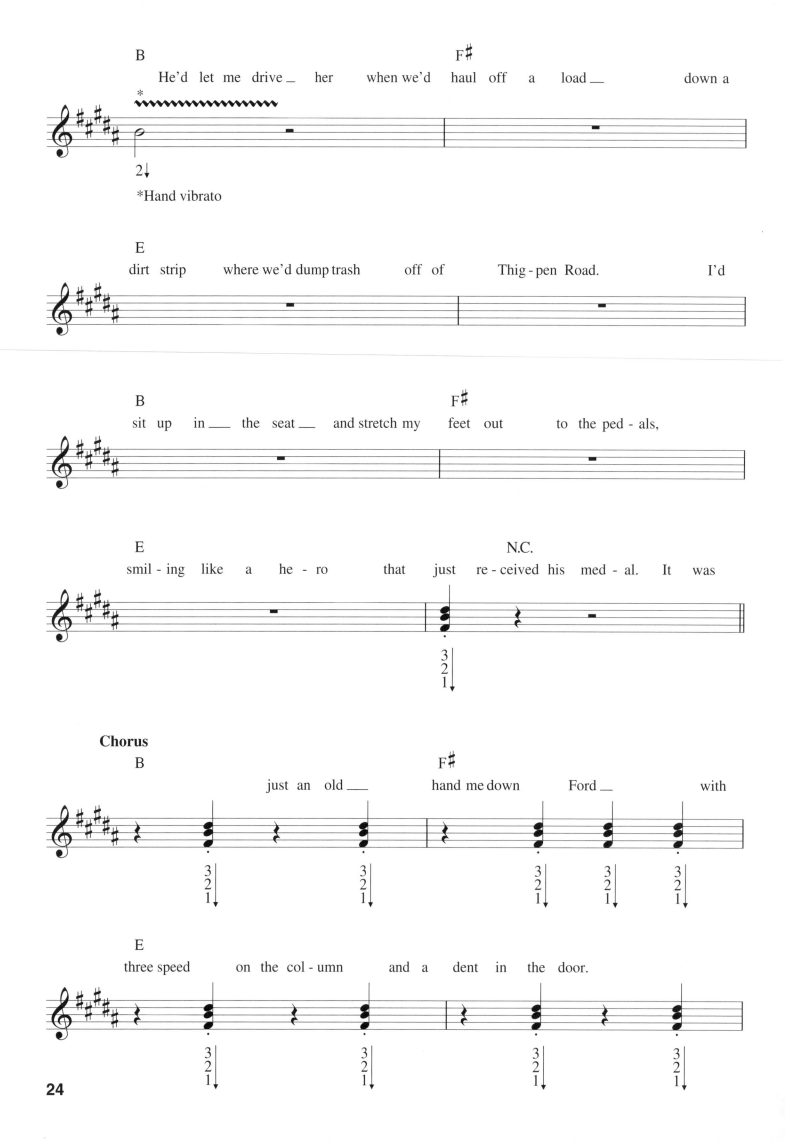

**Interlude**

drive. _____

**Verse**

B                      F#

3. I'm grown up now,     three daugh-ters of my own. ___     I

E

let 'em drive    my old Jeep    'cross the pas - ture at our home.

B                      F#

May-be one day    they'll reach back    in their file     and

E      N.C.                 E      N.C.

pull out that old mem -'ry    and think of me and smile and say, ___

**Chorus**

# Getcha Some

**Words and Music by Toby Keith and Chuck Cannon**

**HARMONICA**

Player: Terry McMilan
Harp Key: C Diatonic

*Throat vibrato throughout
unless indicated otherwise.

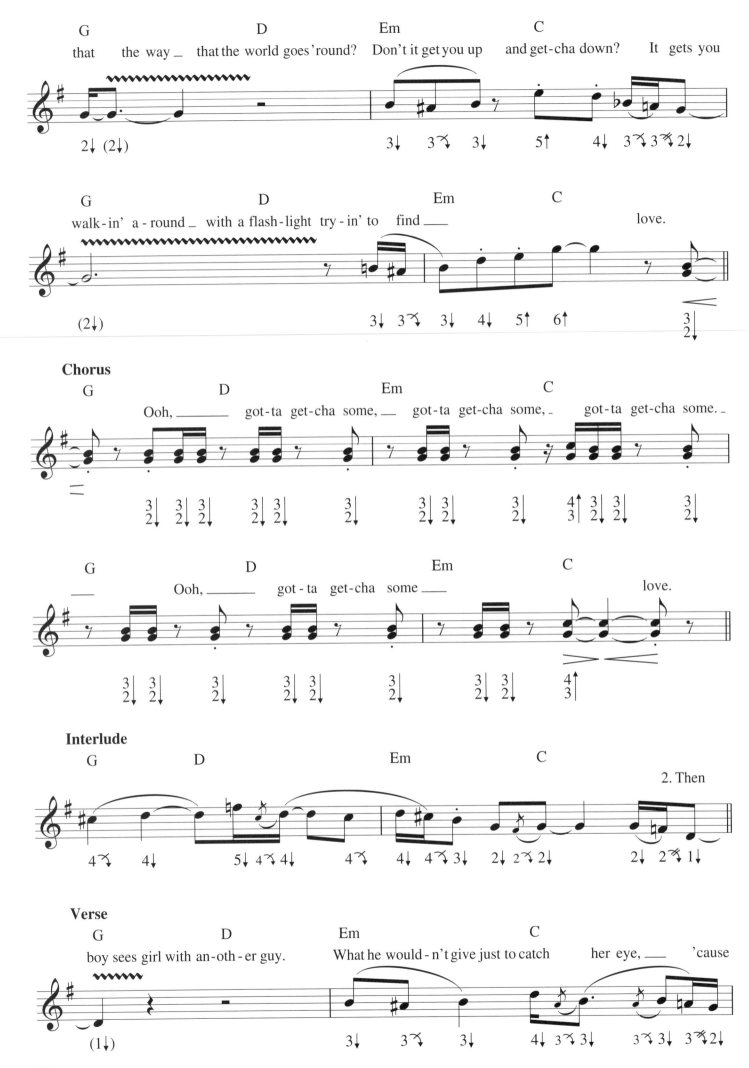

*Tremolo (modulate air flow w/ tongue)

**Chorus**

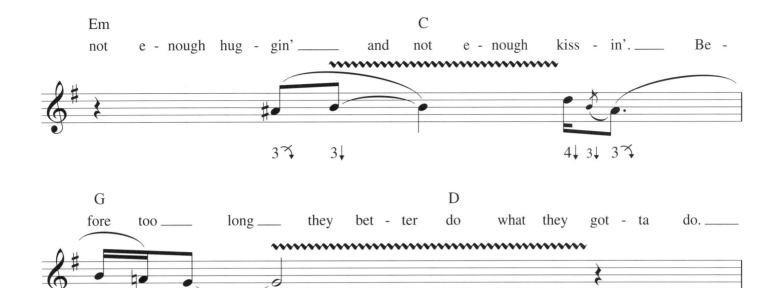

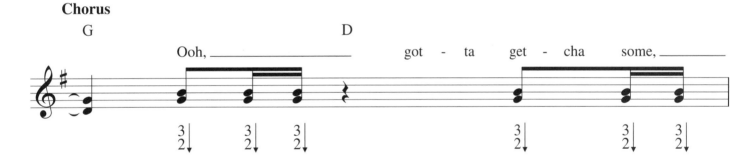

**Chorus**

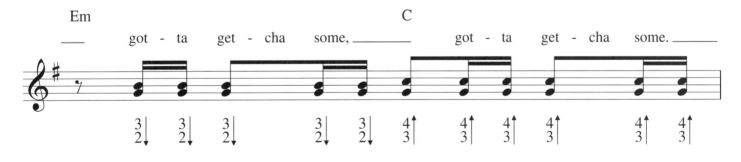

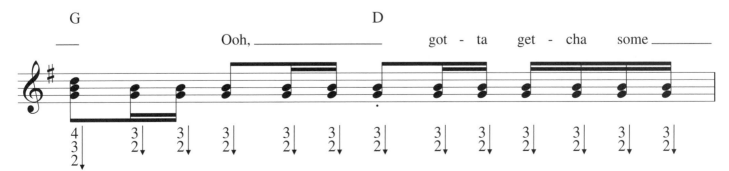

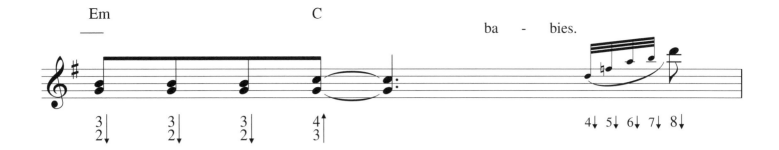

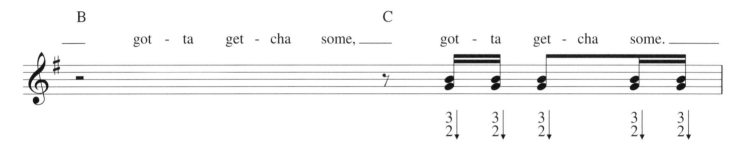

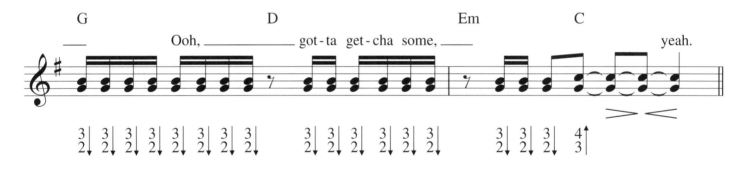

**Outro**

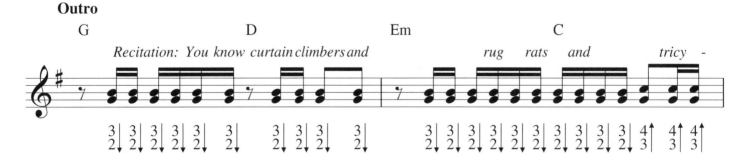

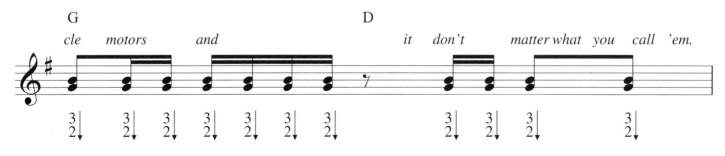

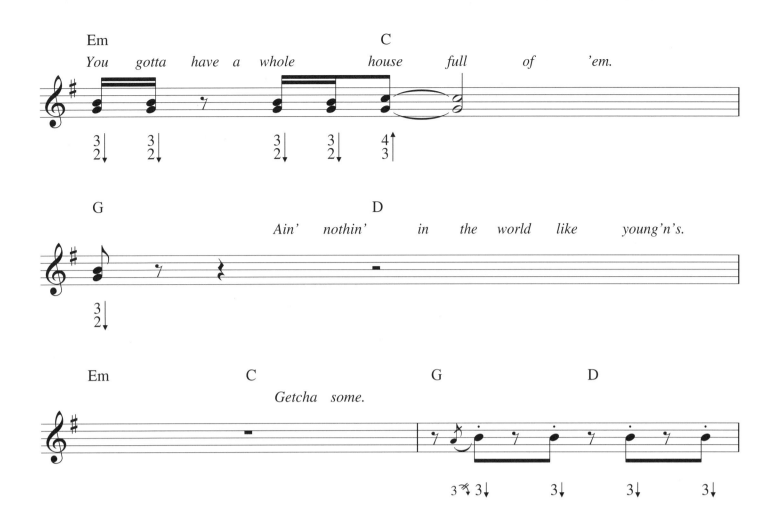

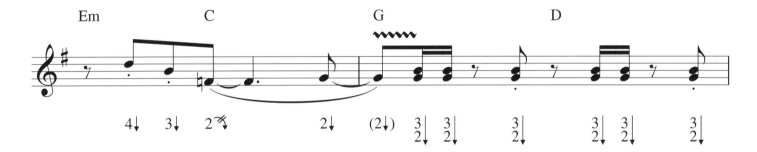

Begin fade

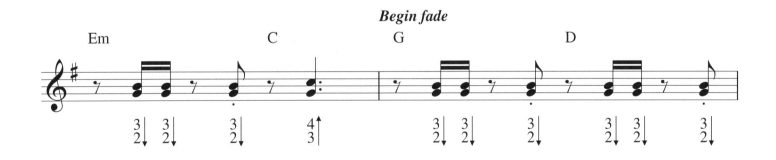

Fade out

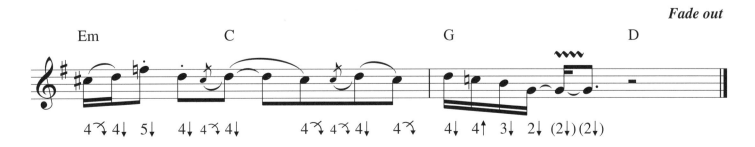

# Here's a Quarter
# (Call Someone Who Cares)

**Words and Music by Travis Tritt**

HARMONICA
Player: Jimmy Joe Ruggiere
Harp Key: C Diatonic

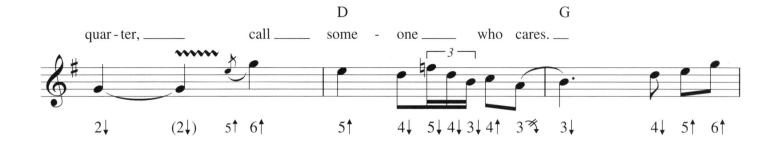

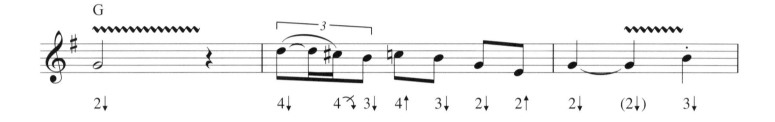

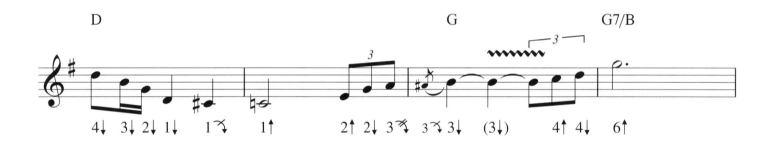

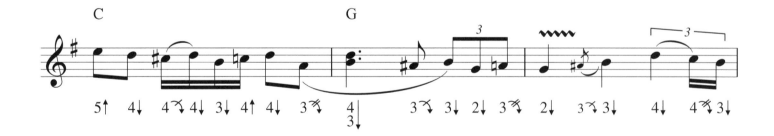

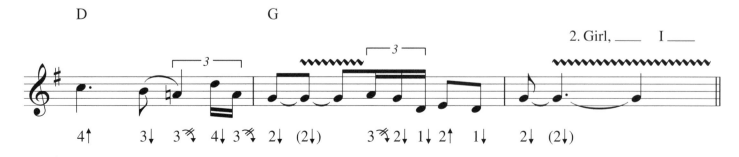

38

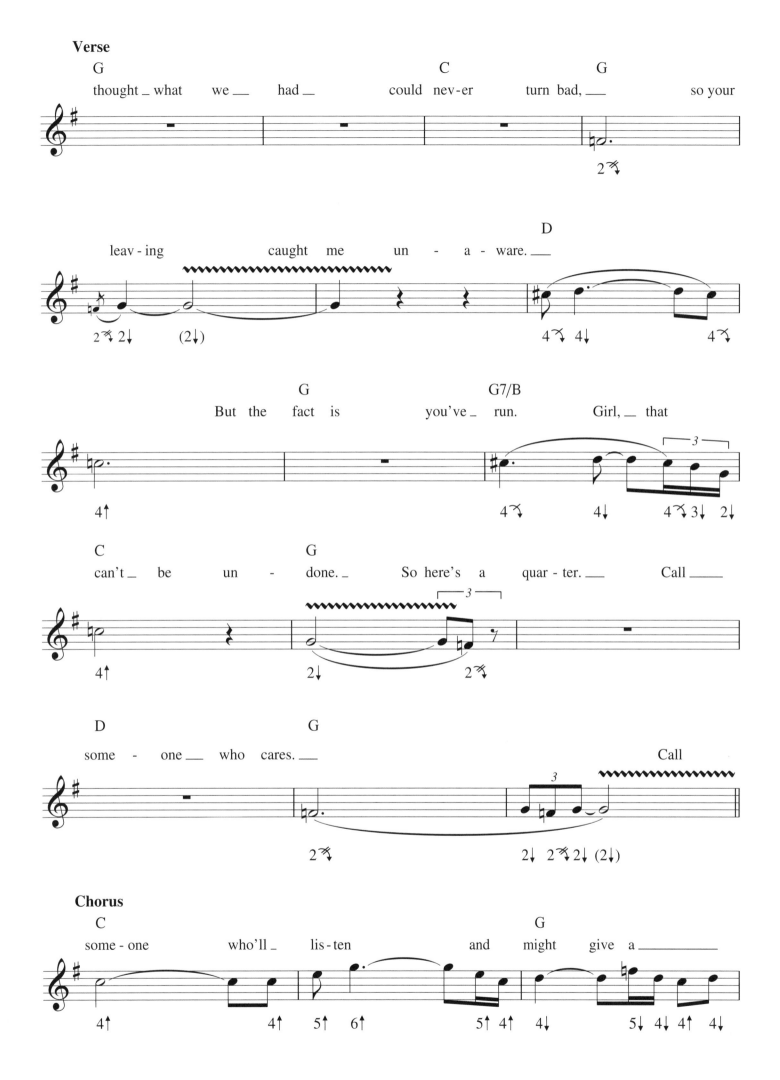

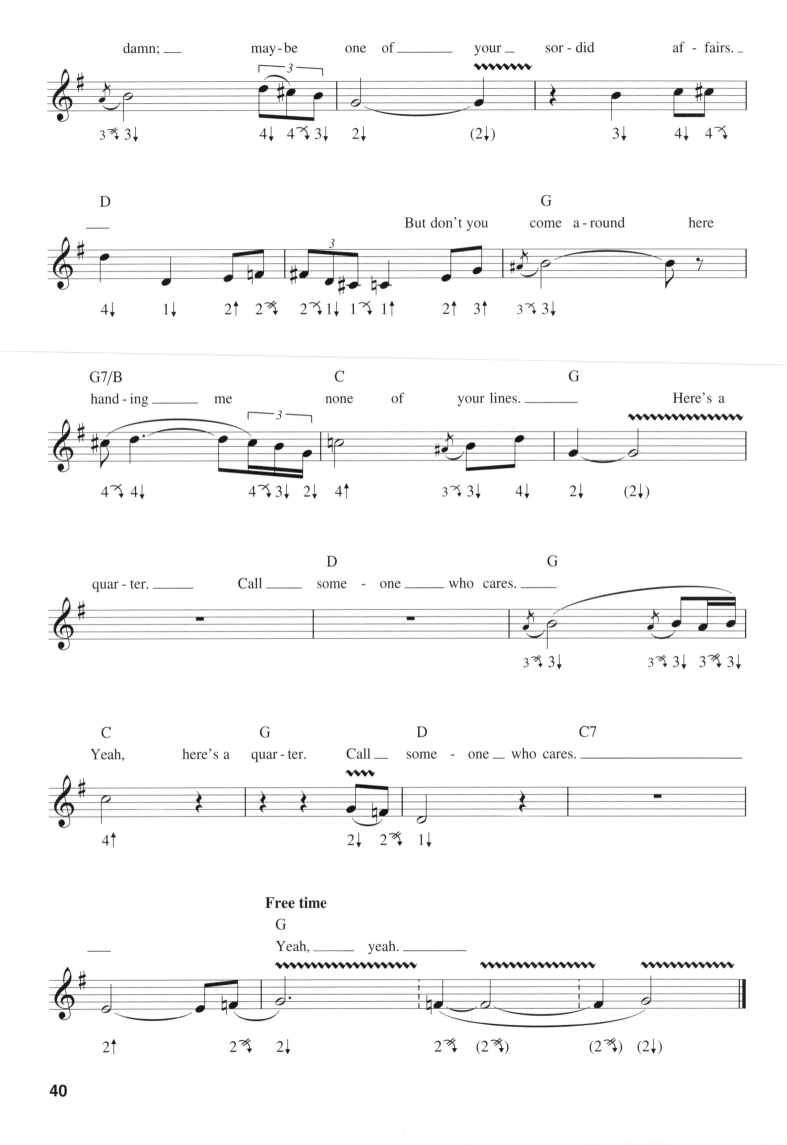

# Put Yourself in My Shoes

**Words and Music by Clint Black,**
**Hayden Nicholas and Shake Russell**

**HARMONICA**

**Player: Clint Black**
**Harp Key: D Diatonic**

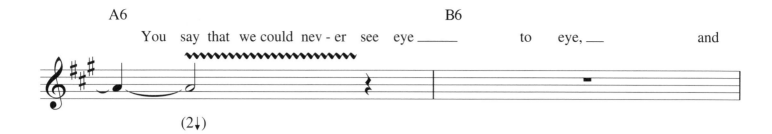

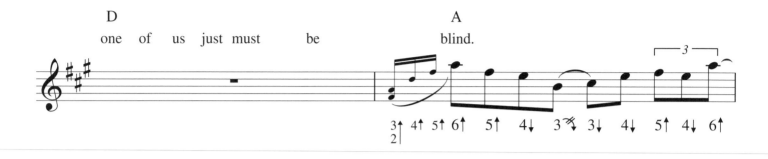

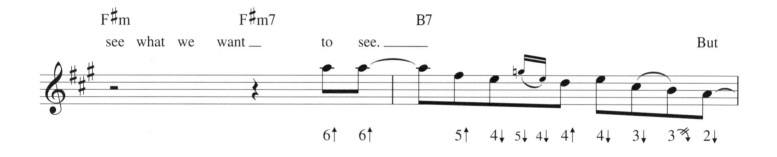

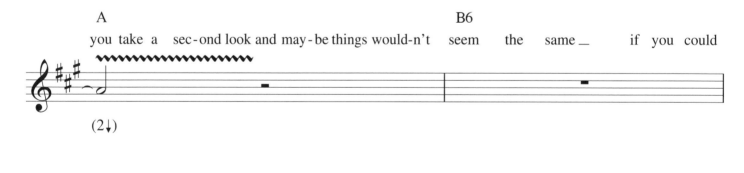

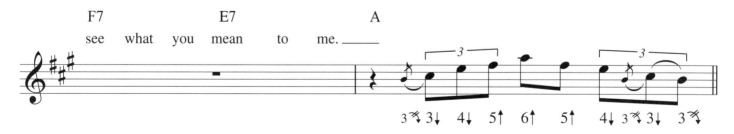

**Chorus**

*Played as even eighth-notes.

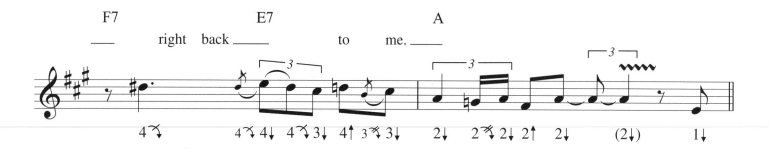

**Interlude**

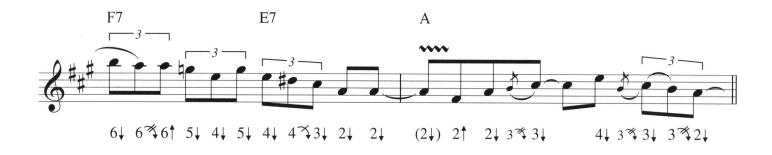

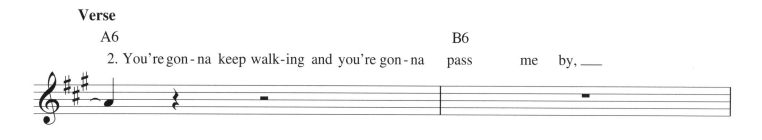

**Verse**

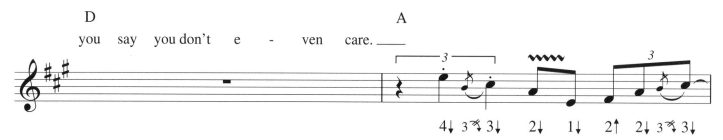

*Sung as even eighth-notes.

**Chorus**

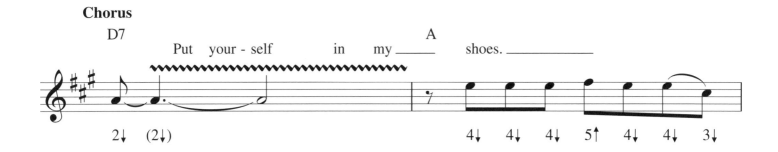

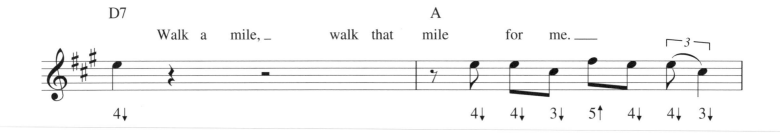

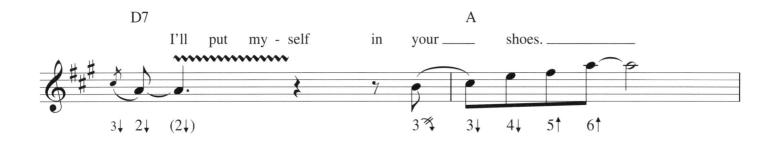

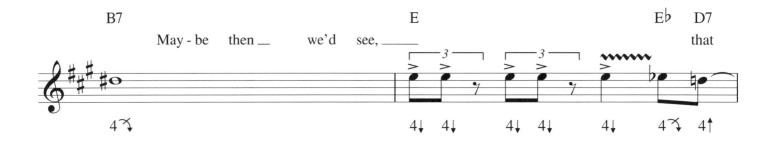

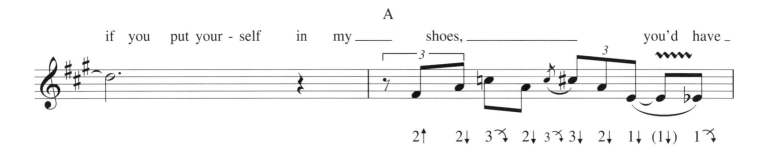

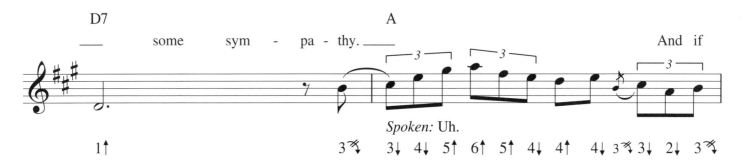

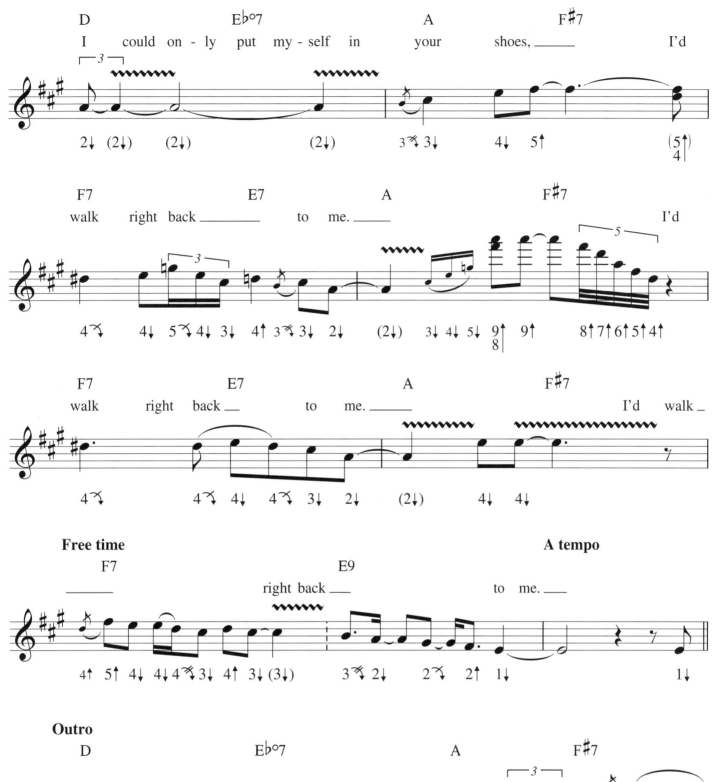

# Honkytonk U

**Words and Music by Toby Keith**

| HARMONICA | | |
|---|---|---|
| **Player:** Mickey Raphael | | |
| **Harp Keys:** G Diatonic | | |
| C Diatonic | | |
| A Diatonic | | |

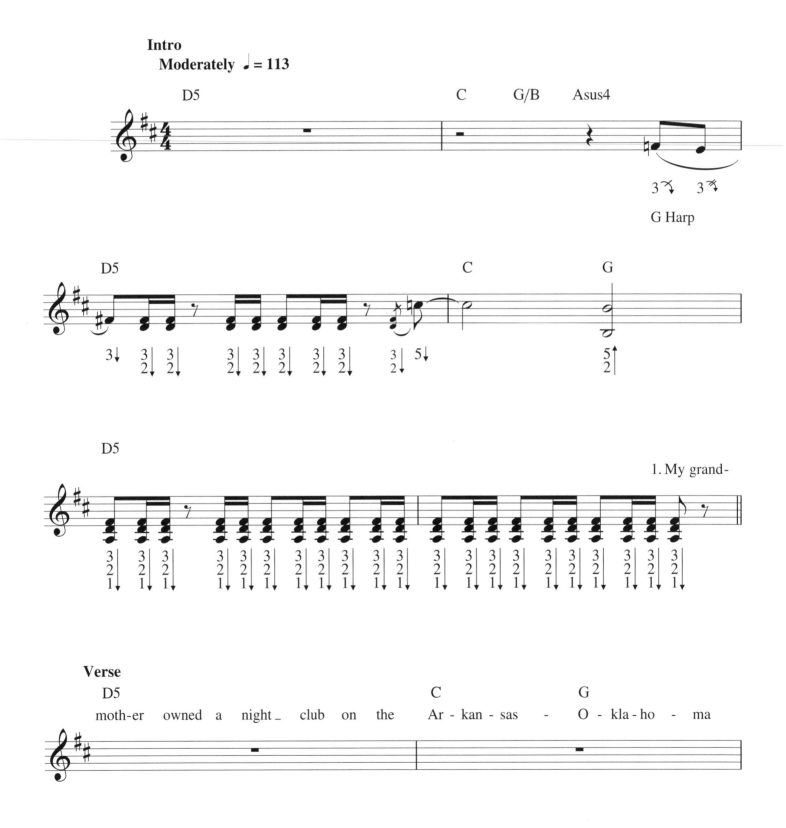

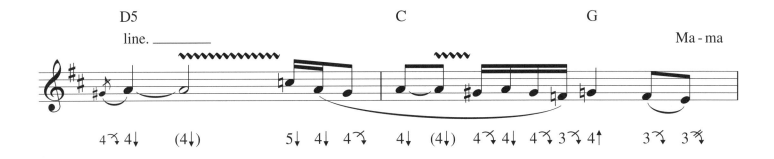

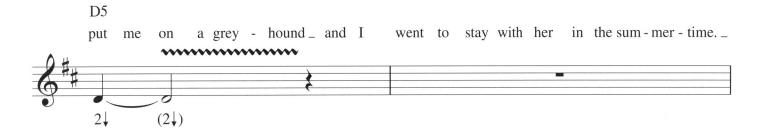

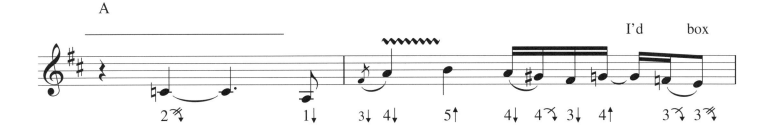

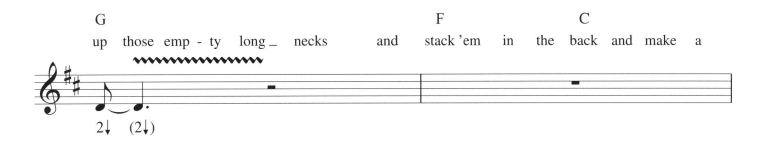

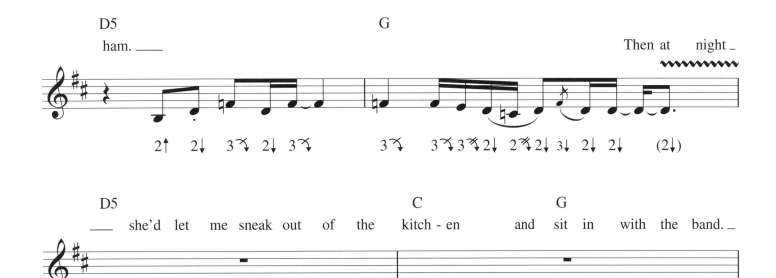

D5

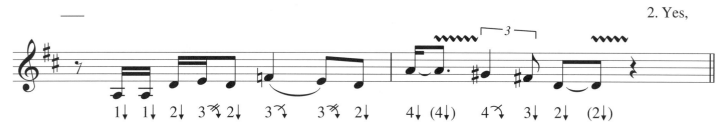

2. Yes,

1↓ 1↓ 2↓ 3↗ 2↓ 3↗ 3↗ 2↓ 4↓ (4↓) 4↗ 3↓ 2↓ (2↓)

**Verse**

D5                         C           G

I have sacked some quar - ter - backs and    broke my share of bones a - long the

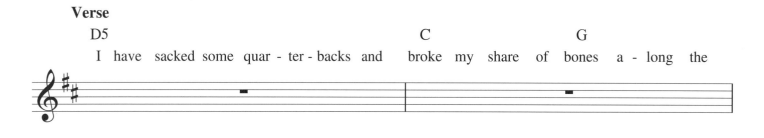

D5                        C           G

way.                                                  I

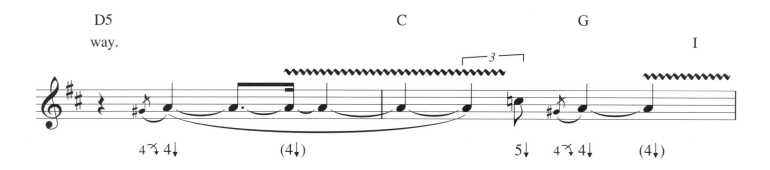

4↗ 4↓        (4↓)                5↓ 4↗ 4↓      (4↓)

D5

knew it would-n't last __ for - ev - er,    sem - i    pro   al - ways means sem - i

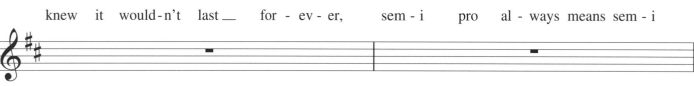

Go to C Harp

A

paid. _____                                            I

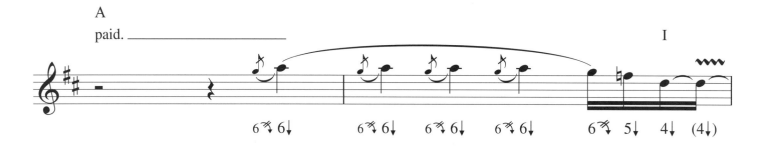

6↗ 6↓      6↗ 6↓    6↗ 6↓    6↗ 6↓     6↗ 5↓ 4↓ (4↓)

G                                     F            C

start - ed climb - ing drill-ing rigs, I'm oil field trash and proud as I can be, __

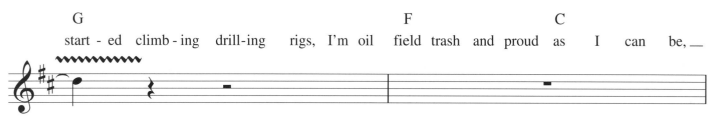

Go to G Harp

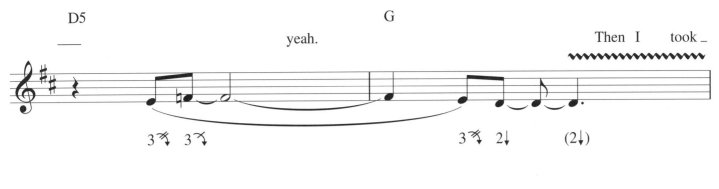

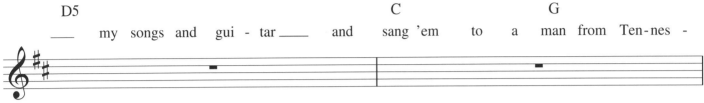

**Chorus**

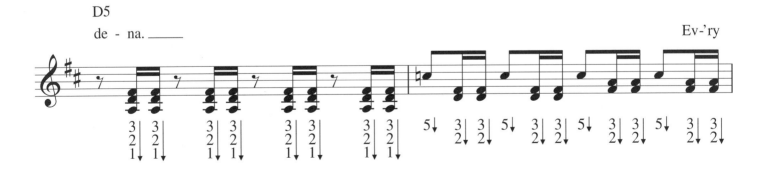

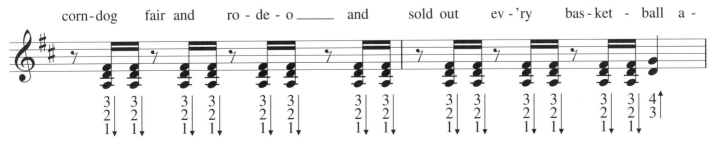

**Verse**

E5                                           D             A

star can't burn for - ev – er    and the    bright-est ones will some-day lose their

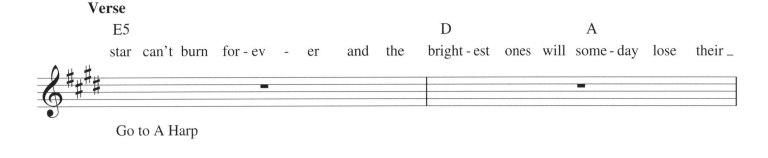

Go to A Harp

E5                                         D             A

shine.                                             But the glass

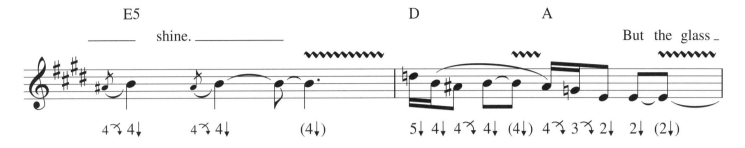

4↗ 4↓      4↗ 4↓     (4↓)     5↓ 4↓ 4↗ 4↓ (4↓) 4↗ 3↗ 2↓  2↓ (2↓)

E5

won't ev - er be        half  emp - ty in  my  op - ti - mis - tic

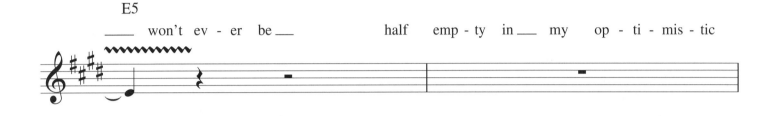

B

mind.

3↓ 4↓ 5↓ 6↗ 6↓     6↗ 5↓ 4↓   (4↓) 4↗ 3↗  4↗  4↓    4↗ 3↗ 2↓  4↑

A                                        G                    D

I'll   still have a song  to sing and a  band to turn it up   and play it

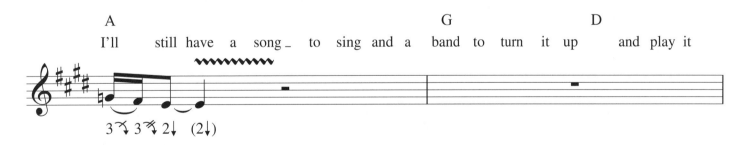

3↗ 3↗ 2↓  (2↓)

E5                                        G           A

loud.                                                  As

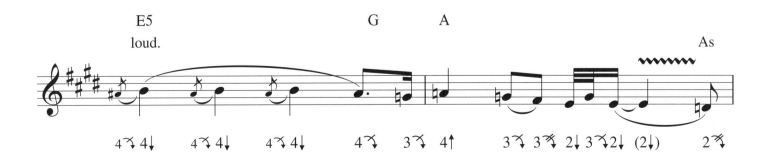

4↗ 4↓    4↗ 4↓    4↗ 4↓    4↗  3↗ 4↑    3↗ 3↗ 2↓ 3↗2↓ (2↓)   2↗

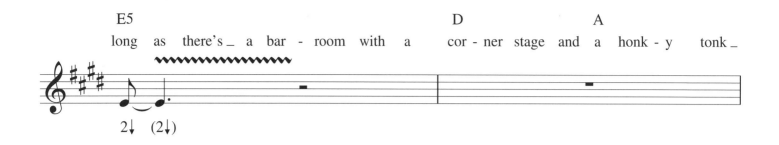

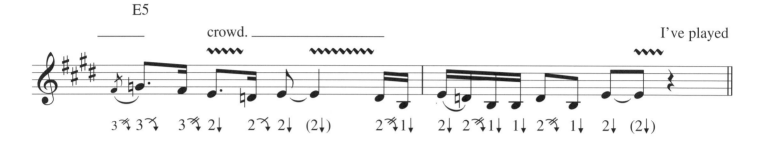

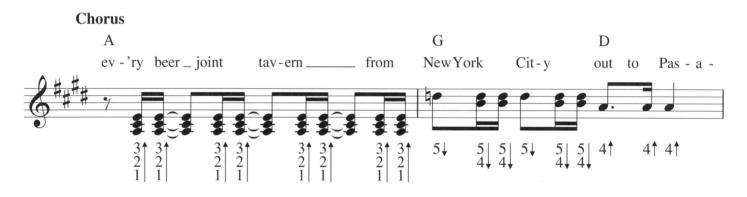

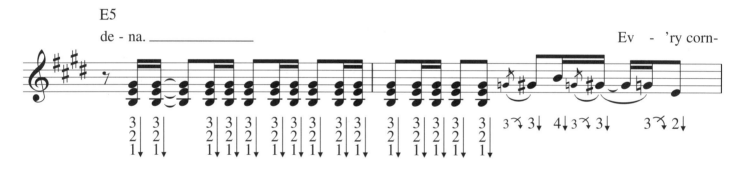

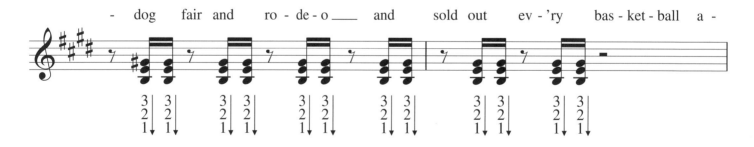

# One More Last Chance

**Words and Music by Gary Nicholson and Vince Gill**

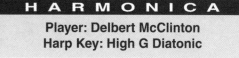

**HARMONICA**
**Player: Delbert McClinton**
**Harp Key: High G Diatonic**

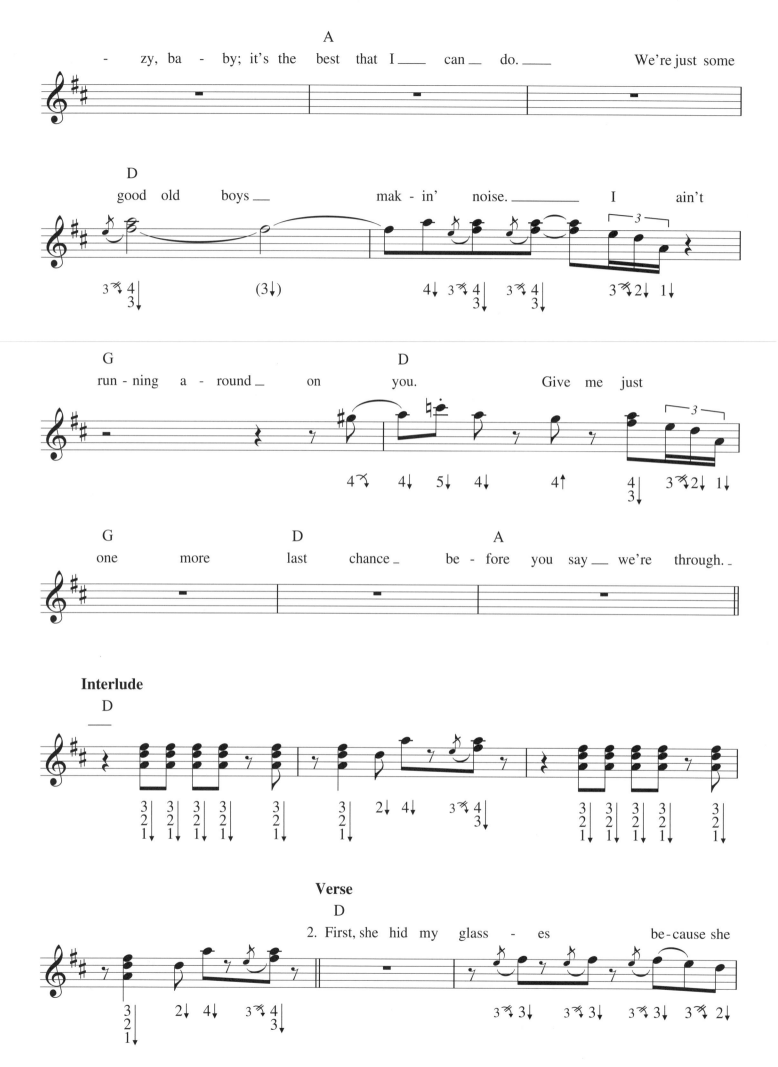

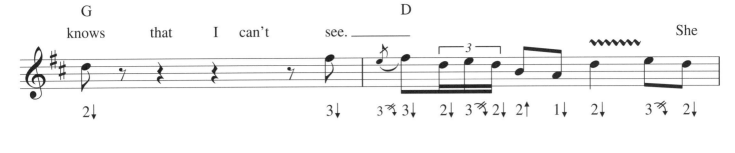

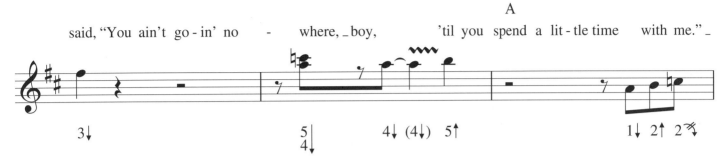

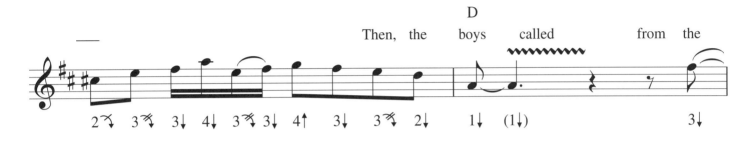

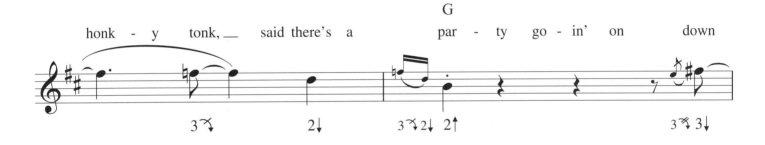

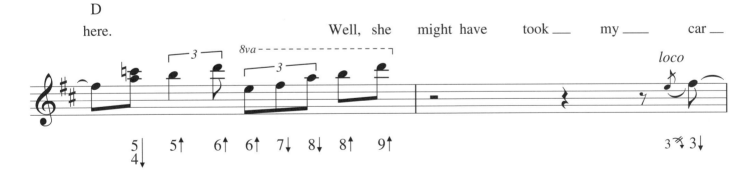

D
Deere.                                                                                                      Give me just

(2↓)        3⤸3↓   2↓   3↓   4↓   5↓   5↑   6↑

**Chorus**

D                                                                          G
one        more            last     chance __   be - fore  you  say __ we're  through. __

3⤸4↓   3⤸4↓        5↓  3⤸4↓      4⤸2↓   (2↓)
3↓       3↓          4↓     3↓         3⤸

D                                                          I    know    I   drive __  you  cra -

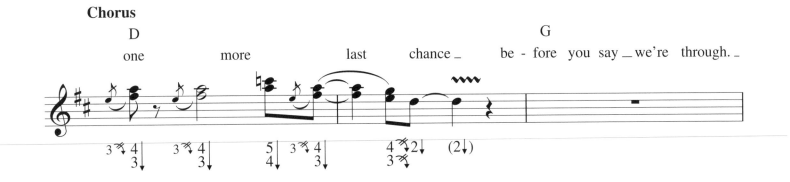

4⤸4↓  5↓   4↓  4⤸3↓   4↑   5↑   3⤸3↓   2↓   (2↓)
4↓

A
- zy,  ba  -  by;  it's  the  best  that  I ___ can __ do. ___        We're just some

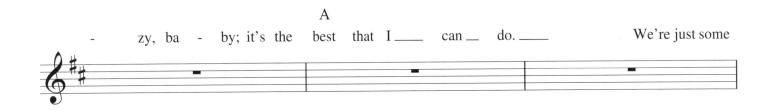

D                                                          G
good old      boys __        mak - in' noise __  I  ain't   run-ning a - round __  on

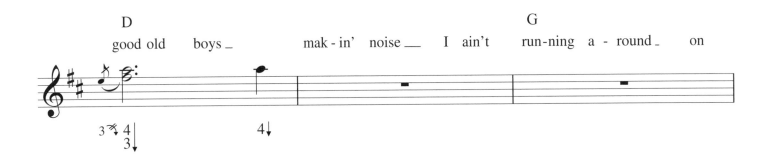

3⤸4↓
3↓
4↓

D                                          G                D
you.              Give me just       one      more        last  chance __  be -

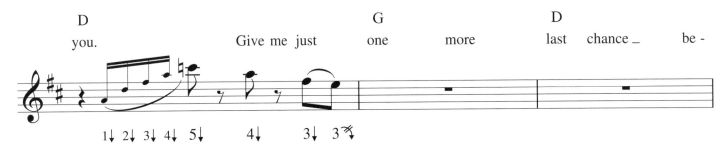

1↓  2↓  3↓  4↓  5↓      4↓      3↓  3⤸

**Interlude**

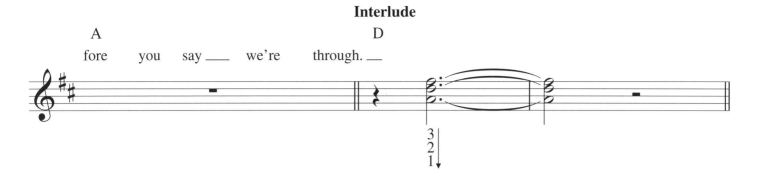

fore you say ___ we're through. ___

**Guitar Solo**

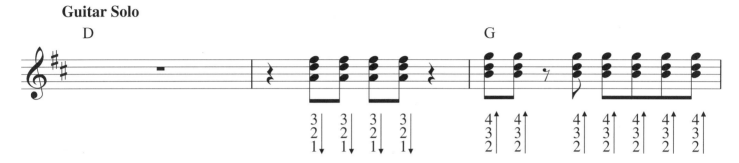

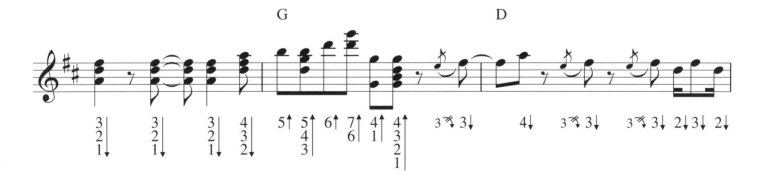

*Tremolo (modulate air flow)

**Chorus**

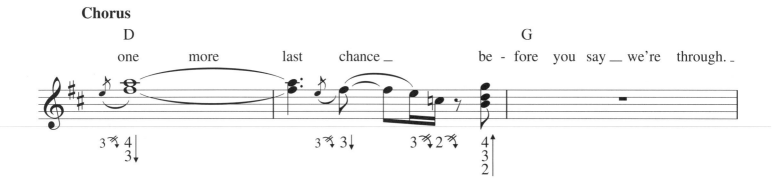

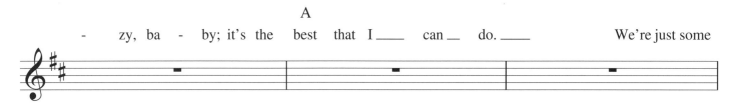

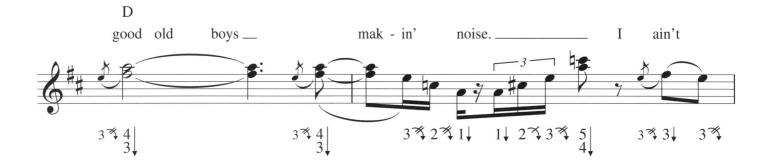

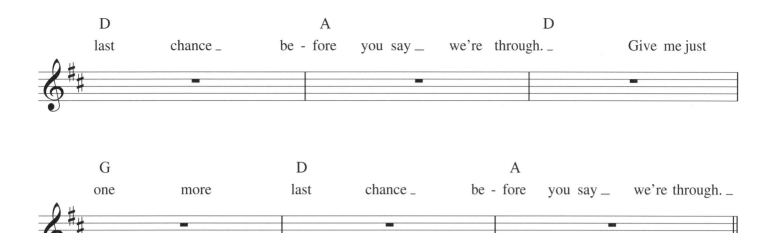

last chance _ be - fore you say _ we're through. _ Give me just

one more last chance _ be - fore you say _ we're through. _

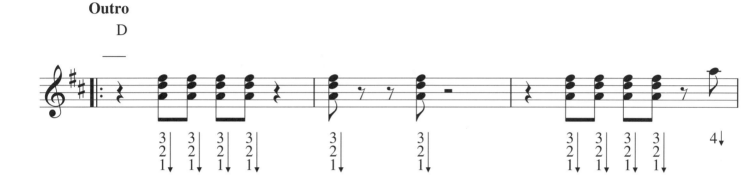

**Outro**

*Begin fade*

*Play 4 times*

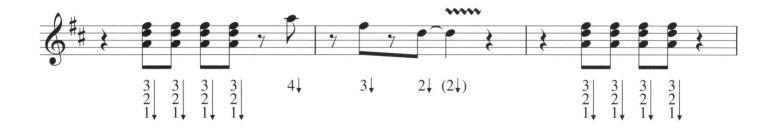

*Fade out*

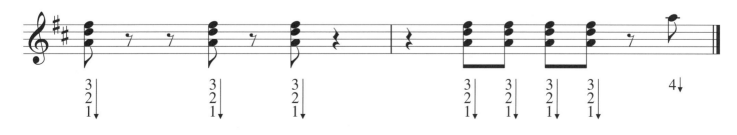

# Turn It Loose

**Words and Music by Don Schlitz,
Brent Maher and Craig Bickhardt**

**H A R M O N I C A**
Player: Kirk "Jelly Roll" Johnson
Harp Key: B Diatonic

**Intro**

**Moderately** ♩ = 120

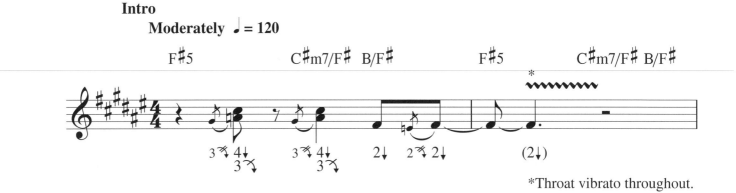

*Throat vibrato throughout.

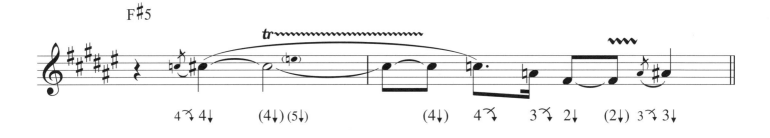

**Verse**

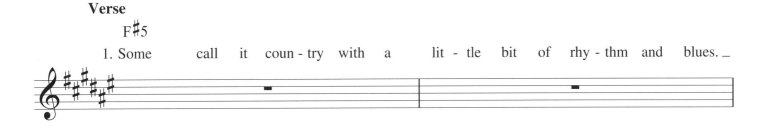

F#5

1. Some call it coun - try with a lit - tle bit of rhy - thm and blues. _

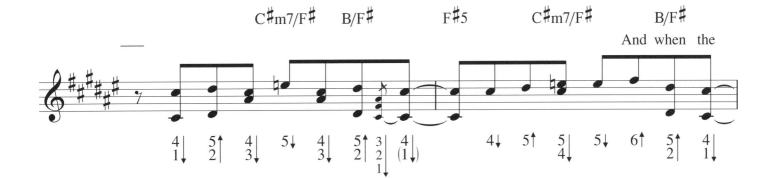

C#m7/F#    B/F#         F#5        C#m7/F#         B/F#

And when the

F#5

boys start rock - ing, there's a beat that you just can't _ lose. _

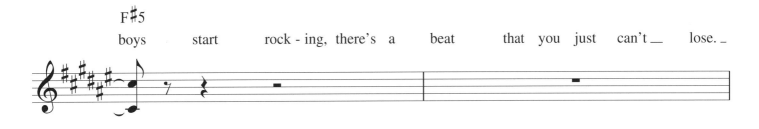

C#m7/F#    B/F#         F#5        C#m7/F#         B/F#

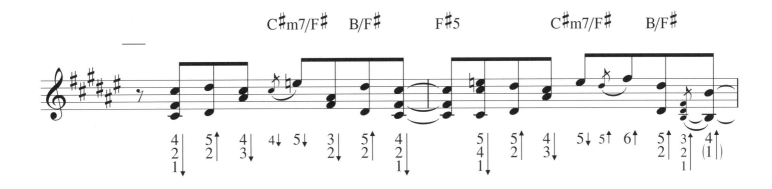

B

Where it's gon - na take us, no - bod - y knows; _ it

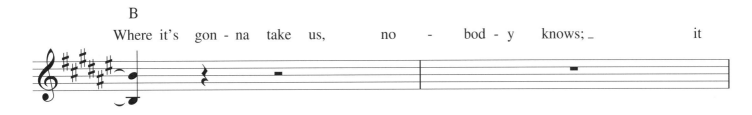

C#7

sure feels good to the bod - y and

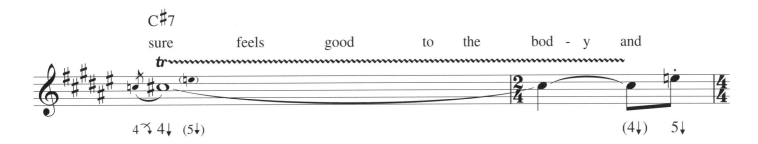

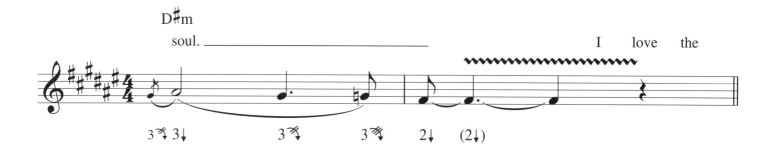

**Chorus**

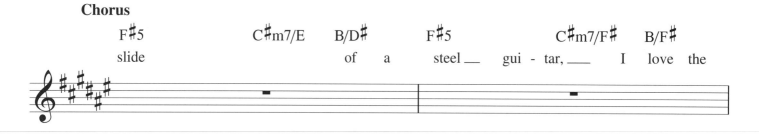

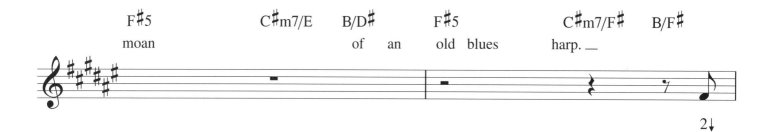

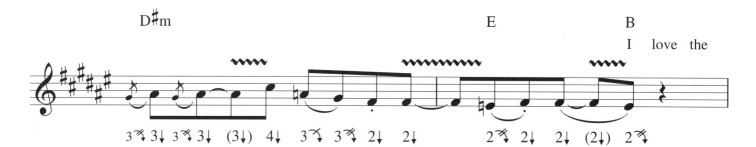

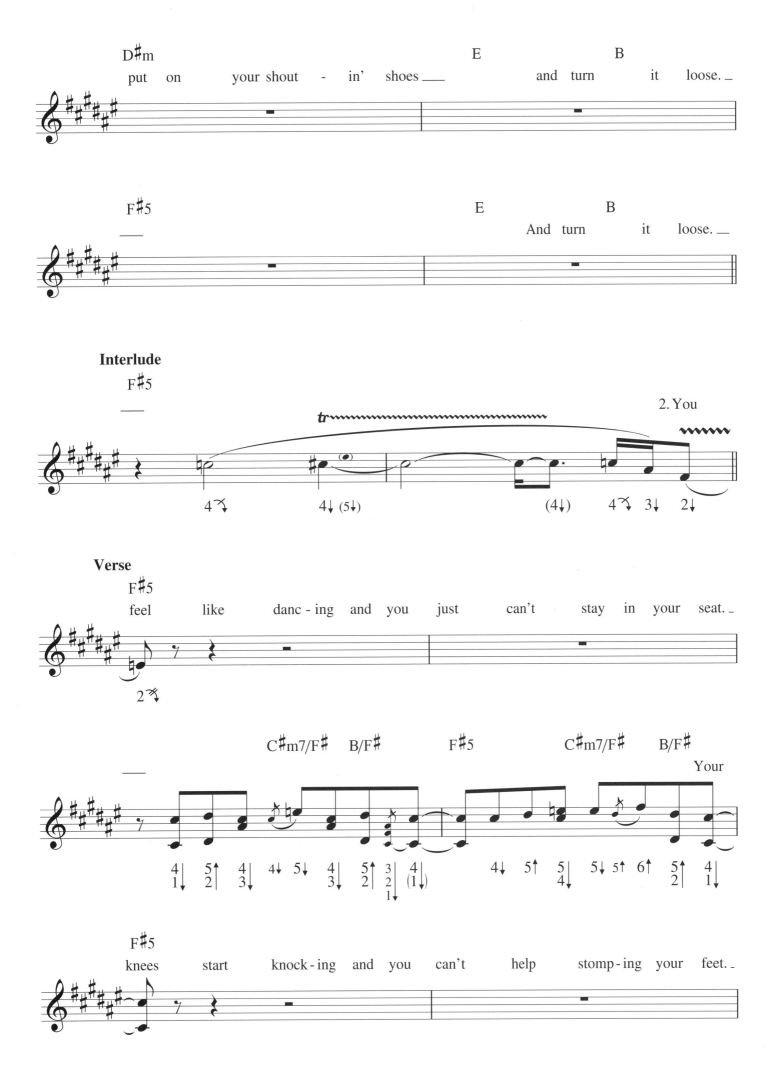

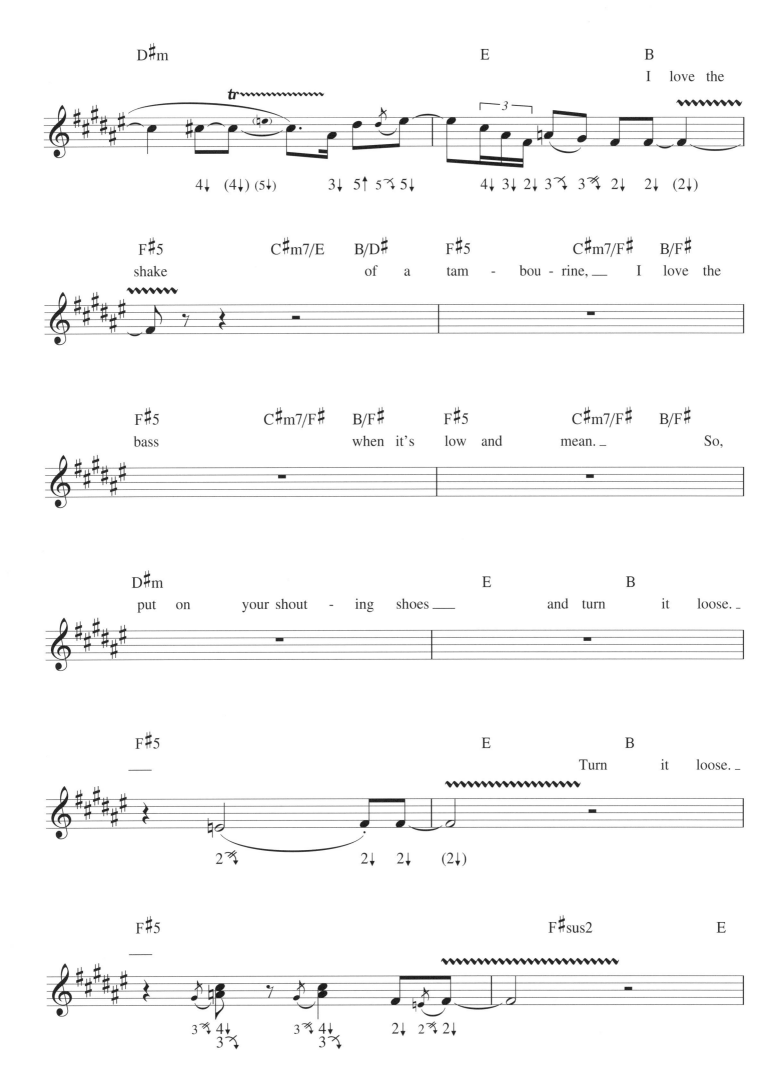

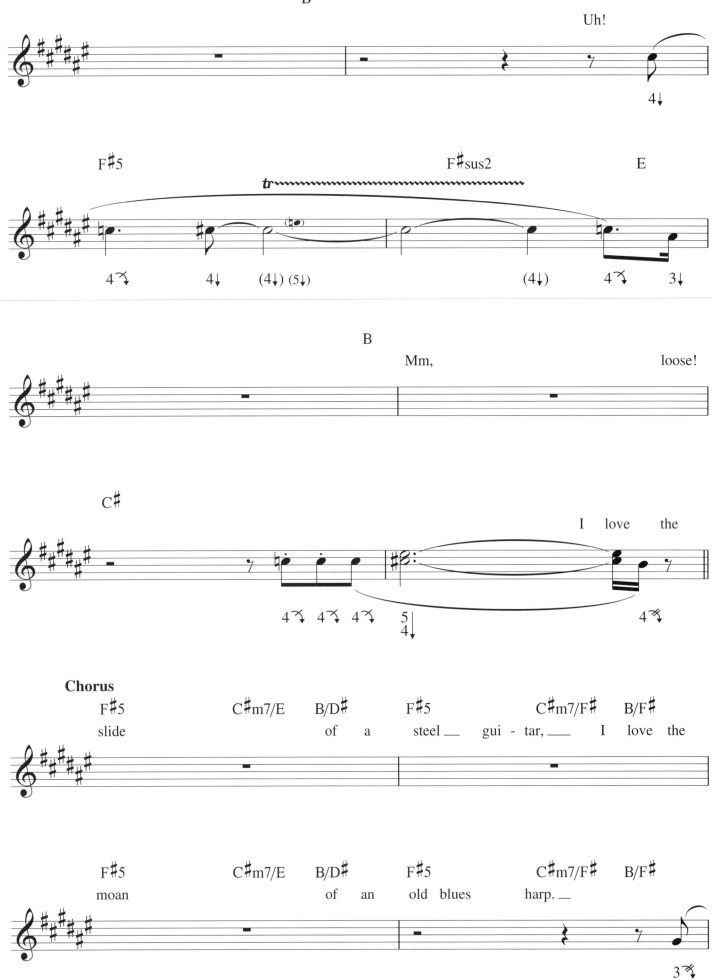

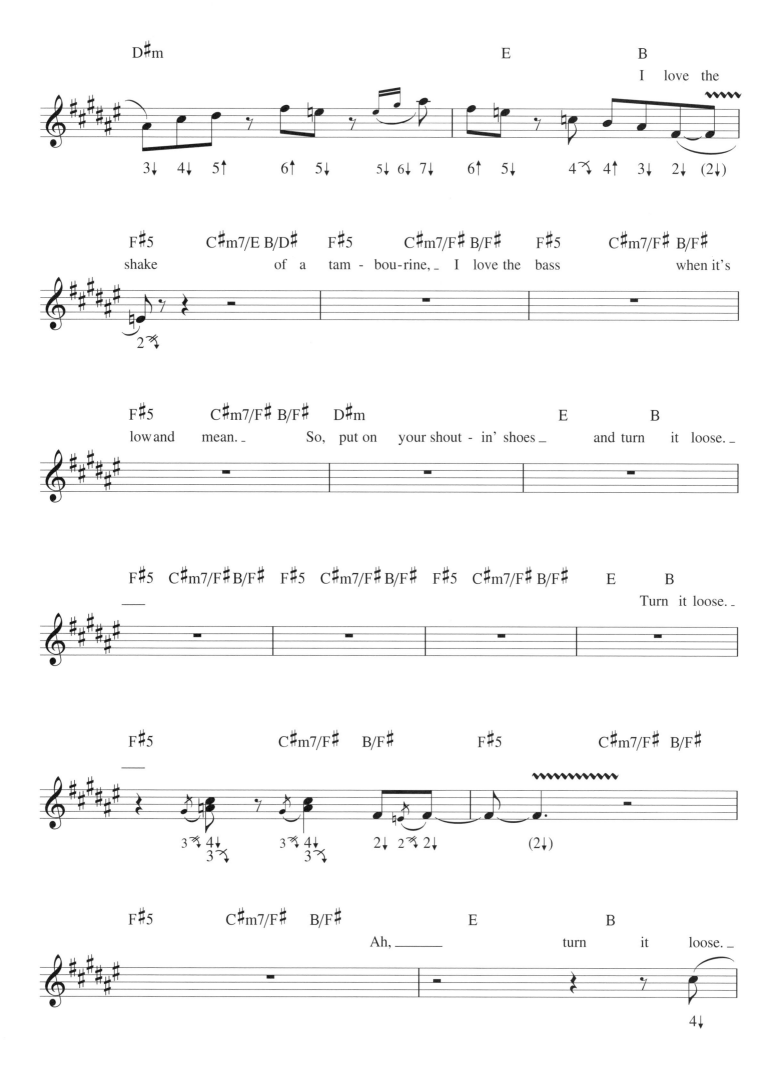

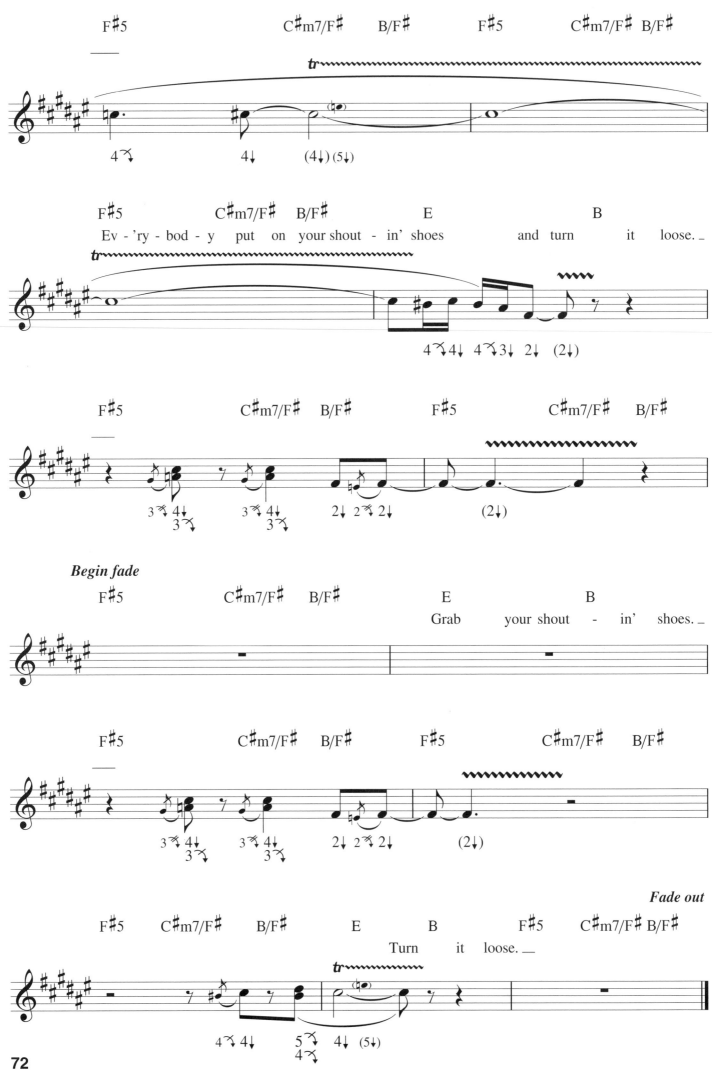